2002

To One "Country Lady"

About Another Country Lady

A great Coffee table Book

For Montana Holidays.

Love Amber

Enjoy your Country Christmas!

Forever Christmas

ALSO BY TASHA TUDOR

Corgiville Fair

The Great Corgiville Kidnapping

The Night Before Christmas

ALSO BY HARRY DAVIS

Tasha Tudor's Dollhouse

The Art of Tasha Tudor

Forever Christmas

Illustrated by
TASHA TUDOR

Written by HARRY DAVIS

PHOTOGRAPHS BY JAY PAUL

Little, Brown and Company
BOSTON   NEW YORK   LONDON

For
James Robert Orum
and
Steven White

We gratefully acknowledge the help of Maureen Orth, Brian Metz, Sara Truitt, and Erik Froehlich in making this book a reality.

Text copyright © 2000 by Harry Davis
Artwork copyright © 2000 by Corgi Cottage Industries
Photographs copyright © 2000 by Jay Paul

First Edition

Library of Congress Cataloging-in-Publication Data

Davis, Harry.
    Forever Christmas / by Harry Davis ; illustrated by Tasha Tudor ; with photographs by Jay Paul.
        p.   cm.
    ISBN 0–316–85542–1
    1. Christmas—Vermont. 2. Tudor, Tasha. I. Title.
GT4986.V5D38   2000
394.2663'09743—dc21   99–35313

10 9 8 7 6 5 4 3 2

TWP

Printed in Singapore

CONTENTS

INTRODUCTION

*"Christmas has always been my family's favorite celebration.
It is a time of magic. Is it not?" — Tasha Tudor*

Tasha Tudor's legendary Christmas celebrations give life to the ultimate fantasies that many of us still cherish in the deep, childlike recesses of our hearts. She has an unusual ability to give every facet of the holiday season a magical quality. On the surface, much of her magic is the ordinary, obtainable variety, but she infuses it with such enthusiasm that the result is always extraordinary.

The wonderful Christmas traditions Tasha created for her own family have been detailed beautifully through more than a score of books and Advent calendars, many hundreds of Christmas cards, and most recently a video. Through these works she has shared her unique approach to Christmas with millions of fans around the world, defining and shaping Christmas in such a way that myth, magic, and mystery have all become part of a celebration that is both secular and religious.

My first encounter with a Tasha Tudor Christmas was through an Advent calendar that, as a child, I had saved up to buy. I found it mesmerizing. Suddenly all my childhood fantasies and beliefs were made credible and real by a name that even sounded mystical: Tasha Tudor. I lived within that calendar during that first December and have returned to it every December since for the past four decades. It presented the world as it should be: all the creatures of the woods living in a sharing, harmonious community, with everyone taking some responsibility for the common good — travel through a snowy forest is made possible by lantern-bearing owls; gnomes glide through the air on white geese; rabbits ski through deep snow, carrying apples for grateful deer; and birds carol by candlelight.

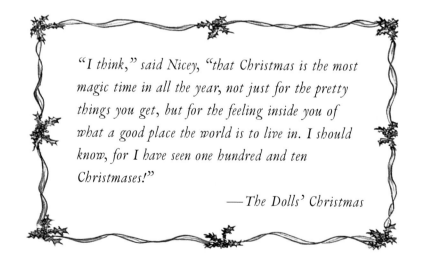

The absolute best part of the calendar, however, shows the world underneath the forest. Burrows teem with life, joy, and celebration. Rabbits have tea around a comforting fireplace; mice inspect a well-stocked larder and dance gleefully under mistletoe. Mother rabbits rock their young to sleep. Raccoons perform merry jigs while toasting one another. Everyone is enjoying bounty, goodwill, and Christmas! I was fascinated by every detail of that calendar. Magic did exist, and it was good.

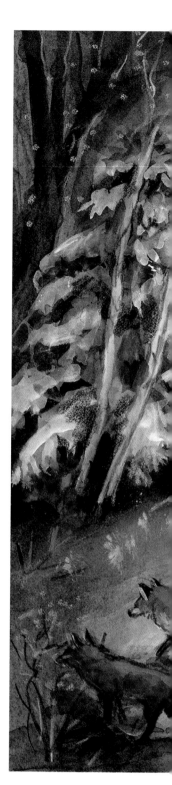

"I think," said Nicey, *"that Christmas is the most magic time in all the year, not just for the pretty things you get, but for the feeling inside you of what a good place the world is to live in. I should know, for I have seen one hundred and ten Christmases!"*

—*The Dolls' Christmas*

ÐREAMRIDE

The intensity of bright moonlight on new-fallen snow is dramatically captured in this painting. The delight on the children's faces is evident as they enjoy a mystical fantasy ride on that most symbolic creature of Christmas, a reindeer. Escorted by foxes, this midnight ride through the forest could be evocative of the most marvelous dreams of childhood or, in Tasha's magical world, could be as simple as the Tudor children hailing an agreeable reindeer for a pleasant ride home.

Until I visited Corgi Cottage many years later, no room had ever seemed as comfortable as those burrows. When I first walked into Tasha's house, I knew I had at last entered the warmth and comfort of the forest burrows. I found a harmonious world where everything had a place and purpose. My first Christmas there would flow into many others, each one unique and different, yet all within the comforting structure of life-long traditions of Advent wreaths, Dundee cakes, Tasha's famous gingerbread ornaments, the late-night search for the Christ child, and Christmas for the animals.

After my first encounter with Tasha's Advent calendar, I began to collect her Christmas books. Her classic *Becky's Christmas* introduced me to the Tudor family's Christmas traditions, and I was enchanted. *Snow Before Christmas* reminded me of my own extended family and gave validity to my rural upbringing. Christmas and Tasha Tudor became inseparable in my mind.

Each of Tasha's Christmas traditions is perfectly staged and timed, allowing for both anticipation and unhurried enjoyment of the moment. As Tasha explains, "Sometimes anticipating something is equal to its actually happening." That is her first, most important lesson for a pressured, fast world where overscheduling and getting things done are considered virtues. Tasha has taught me to enjoy the thoughts of good times to come and to truly experience them as they happen, making each one last as long as possible.

As in all homes, Christmas at Corgi Cottage continues to evolve. As children and grandchildren grow into adulthood, customs change, divide, and subdivide. Sometimes new customs take the place of the old.

In terms of calendar years, Tasha Tudor is approaching the winter of a long and fulfilling life. Far from settling into dormancy, however, she continues to evolve in terms of creativity, exploration, curiosity, and joy for the taking. Winter to Tasha is not only the well-deserved enjoyment of a quiet season but also the prelude to the joys of yet another spring. The cycle is as eternal as the legendary magic she continues to create. Her message is as simple as it is wise:

Take Joy!

WINTER AT CORGI COTTAGE

Tasha loves the serenity and calmness of the winterscape of Corgi Cottage when the snow measures over three feet and envelops everything in a soft beauty. The delicate play of light on snow has an ethereal quality that fascinates Tasha.

Advent

Advent is an important time in Tasha's Christmas celebration. It officially begins for the Tudor household on December 6, the birthday of Saint Nicholas. This day, significant in itself, also heralds every coming event of the Christmas season for Tasha and her family.

Tasha herself makes the Advent wreath. Although many tasks are shared with family and friends, this one is Tasha's alone. She has been making Advent wreaths for more than forty years. The pleasure she takes in this longtime ritual is obvious. As with any artist or craftsperson, she chooses the necessary materials carefully. Only the best pieces of boxwood will do. "I used to make it out of spruce or ferns or whatever might be available, but since I always hung it over the long table in the winter kitchen, the shedding needles became a problem. I've made it of boxwood ever since those needles tried to become part of Christmas dinner." A sturdy old wire frame that Tasha is long practiced in using is produced. With deft movements, she forms the wreath slowly, as the boxwood is woven around the frame. "It's easy to make a nice wreath if you concentrate on the fullness of it. You make a base with the long pieces of boxwood, weaving them in and out of the wire frame. You keep adding to it so it looks nice and fluffy, and, of course, you have to make it prettiest on the bottom part because you only see the bottom when you hang it up."

Tasha uses the making of the Advent wreath as her personal entry into this joyous season. Her face becomes more animated as the wreath takes its final shape. Lovingly, reverently she takes out the antique satin ribbons on which half a century of Advent wreaths have hung. A subtle shade of soft red, they are real satin and were first used as pew markers at her mother and father's wedding in 1904.

These same ribbons have had a splendid career since that wedding. Tasha has used them countless times in her book illustrations, calendars, and Christmas cards. Because all of Tasha's art is conceived and created from her life, her art and her life have gradually become virtually indistinguishable.

The ribbons are adjusted and the wreath finished. Tasha trims the base of the candles so they fit snugly into the holders. She uses only her own hand-dipped candles, made from pure beeswax. She nimbly stands on a chair and slips the wreath into place. The hook that holds it has always been there and knows its function. The lighting of the wreath will wait for tea.

Tasha's Advent teas are memorable, none more so than the one on Saint Nicholas's birthday. Her Dundee cakes are the great attraction. Somewhat like a fruitcake, but white, they have appeared on her tea table on this day all her life. Because it's his favorite, Tasha's older son, Seth, gets one all for himself. The recipe came from her beloved Scottish nanny, Dady. It was originally Dady's mother's recipe in Scotland. The cakes were made weeks ago and frozen to improve their taste. Once you've had Tasha's Dundee cake, it remains imprinted on your taste buds, and by mid-November you find yourself anxious that Tasha will once again find time to create one of these culinary masterpieces.

Everything about the tea is relaxed and conducive to the Christmas mood. Lighting the wreath brings forth exclamations of pleasure and congratulations on yet another beautiful creation. "I think when it's done properly, you light only one candle the first week, and two the second, and so on. It was so beautiful, I just lit them all at once and have done so ever since! One should

always feel free to alter traditions when one sees fit."

Tasha's own blend of Welsh breakfast tea, the Dundee cake, and a variety of Christmas cookies induce a sense of well-being. The combination of firelight and candlelight creates a warm glow that gently embraces the entire room. The wreath makes shadows on the ceiling that Tasha describes as "halos of quivering rays." Hanging the Advent wreath introduces one of Tasha's favorite elements of Christmas: the smells. Over the next few weeks, garlands and fresh greens will be brought into the house, filling it with cold, fresh scents. They are important to Tasha. She feels that "scent is the strongest memory arouser. Even more than sight or sound. Balsam fir always reminds me of Christmas." Tasha revels in these and all scents of everyday life — drying mittens, wood smoke, and baking. "Were one to smell any of these things again in a far country, many years hence, the entire scene would come poignantly alive once more and clutch the heart."

In the past, a new Advent calendar was made each year. They were amazingly detailed creations, very much like the one that introduced me to Tasha Tudor. The topics were numerous, from snowy forests to Victorian streets. All were filled with enchanting animals going about daily business. Great glee and contentment always seemed to be the dominant theme, and the work was enormously complex and layered. Underneath the forest floor would be animal burrows; underneath them would be smaller mouse burrows with intricately detailed tiny spaces. Closest to Tasha's heart are the calendars associated with Corgiville, her personal favorite of all her literary and artistic creations. Corgiville, that delightful village "west of New Hampshire and east of Vermont" has its own Christmas celebrations. These fetes are somewhat boisterous, given Tasha's fondness for bogarts, her adaptation of Swedish trolls. One famous calendar was made "just for the boys." "It was rather naughty," concedes Tasha. All the calendars have tiny

Christmas in Corgiville has been the subject of a number of Tasha's Advent calendars. Their peaceful and joyful celebrations mirror many of Tasha's own at Corgi Cottage. Others are simply the way things are done in Corgiville.

doors, twenty-four of them, to be opened, one each day, from December 1 to December 24. Tasha had the children take turns opening the doors. Behind each door would be a tiny scene of Christmas celebration. The last door, to be opened on Christmas Eve, usually revealed the Christ child.

In recent years, with her children grown with families of their own, Tasha produces Advent calendars more slowly. Frequently the originals are away at museum exhibitions, but the combined memory of them seems to permeate the walls of the winter kitchen whether they are there or not. A rich sense of peaceful joyousness remains. Peace on earth is possible, and it extends to all creatures.

"I think scent is the strongest memory arouser. Even more than sight or sound. Balsam fir always reminds me of Christmas."

Gifts

Gift-giving is a serious commitment at Corgi Cottage. Many Christmas presents are handmade and may be worked on all year. "We always spent the summer making presents because we tried to make everything we gave away. That's why I had the big Christmas chest. We kept them there."

All Tasha's children were aware of the uniqueness of handmade gifts. "They made little animals, they all whittled quite well. Seth used to make wooden things. He made the dolls a wonderful croquet set. I still have it. We used to set it up in the parlor and play croquet. The girls used to make knitted facecloths. When Tom and Efner were much younger, Bethany and I would make clothes for their bears and dolls."

Jams and jellies were also made in the summer. Much closer to Christmas, dozens of cookies and candies would be made for gifts. Tasha's parents, William Starling Burgess and Rosamond Tudor, taught her, by example, that in making someone a gift, you gift them twice, once in the doing and again in the gift itself. "Papa used to make wonderful little steam engines that would actually pump steam for the boys. And little cannons that really fired. Of course, Christmas was made even more magical by the fact that it was his birthday. Mamma used to make him immense cakes."

One of Tasha's favorite gifts as a child was a dollhouse made by her mother. "Mamma spent the whole summer making me a dollhouse. When I first saw it, it was amazing, all lighted with birthday candles. It had a front yard with a picket fence made out of meat skewers with pointed ends, painted white. She made all of the furniture. Little rush-bottom chairs made of raffia. It was really amazing to see."

Even in early childhood, Tasha knew her own mind. Cooking was important to her. "Much to my dismay, Mamma made the dining room one half of the house. The kitchen was very small — in back — and it bothered me because it was hard for me to get to and I thought it should be the most important room. I changed it around and made the large room into the kitchen. Mamma didn't mind. She just

wasn't as interested in cooking as I was."

The Tudor family's daily life has always appeared in Tasha's art. Making handmade gifts forms an integral part of one of Tasha's Christmas classics, *Becky's Christmas:*

Becky's family made all their own Christmas presents, except for a few stocking things, which were of course supplied by Santa Claus and not made at home. . . .

So now spare minutes and nearly every evening were spent in making presents. The house was full of surprises, and each person had a private place where absolutely no *other members of the family could come. . . .*

Every afternoon, just about, there would be cooky-making, for a box went to each of their friends and family, and that meant a lot of cookies to be cut and baked and sent away.

Tasha's homemade cheeses, flavored with a variety of herbs, are highly cherished gifts. Months in the making, they are a source of pride and pleasure, as she experiments with different flavors.

Tasha still continues her tradition of handmade gifts. No last-minute shopping sprees exist in Tasha's world. Christmas gifts are made early, whenever possible. If the proposed gift is a lengthy project, it must be started early enough to allow unhurried anticipation of the finished piece and pleasant expectations of how surprised the recipient might be. Fortunate indeed is the family member or friend who receives a hand-knitted pair of socks, jams and jellies, a small drawing, or anything at all from Tasha's hands.

HARVEST PANTRY

As Christmas nears, jams, jellies, and preserves, as well as cookies and candies, await their mailing to family friends. The storehouse quality of Tasha's ample pantry is beautifully presented here, with all of Tasha's favorite kitchenware forming a bountiful backdrop.

Opposite page:
Tasha loves to carve and has plans to make a complete ark. Here, some of her wooden animals join their counterparts in an illustration from Tasha's newest version of The Night Before Christmas.

SUGAR COOKIES

The typical industry of Tasha's winter kitchen is beautifully depicted in this painting. Tasha usually uses the end of this harvest table as her studio, but cookie making is an art in itself, so she relinquishes it when necessary.

Snow

"I like the smell of snow. Snow has a definite smell, like apple blossoms, oddly enough. Usually you can tell when snow is coming by the smell in the air."

Tasha is quite fond of snow. Its primary purpose is to ensure a good garden. But, equally, she enjoys the beauty of falling snow. The light reflected off snow is a source of continual fascination to her, and she has worked hard and successfully to capture it in her watercolors. The feeling of comfort and snugness that snow up to the windowsill can induce is also greatly in its favor. When deep snow has enveloped Corgi Cottage and it becomes a world unto itself, the silence is palpable: it can be heard and felt, almost seen. Time ceases to exist.

Tasha is not one simply to look at the snow; she must be out in it. She finds great beauty in the smallest detail. "Birds make such beautiful patterns, like lace, in the snow." On snowshoes she reaches distant woods where desirable greens are still obtainable for wreaths and garlands. The journey in the snow makes her recall pleasures from the past. "My friend Rose and I used to be fond of the snow and rather adventurous. Once we built an igloo and slept for several nights in it with her cat, Puddings. The snow horses were my favorite, though. Rose and I made them quite large; children could actually ride them. We would pour water on them and they would freeze and become very slippery, and you could slide up and down on their backs. They would last a long time."

I suddenly remember a scene similar to the one she is describing. It's from Tasha's *Snow Before Christmas* and is one of my favorite illustrations. I seek out the book and show it to Tasha. She smiles, remembering, and encourages us to try our hand at it. "Wouldn't it be fun to make them again?" We do, and shortly before darkness sets in, several stand icy sentinel in a wide field of snow. By twilight they seem mysterious and unapproachable. We admire them from afar, half expecting shadow children to gleefully mount their backs.

A newer but equally charming custom is that of the snow lanterns. Tasha learned the art from a friend, Linda Allen. It is a Scandinavian tradition that easily became a Tudor one. At tea, Tasha describes the process:

"You make snowballs — you have to have the right kind of snow, wet — and you have to put them together in a circle and build them up and up and up until you make an igloo. You leave a space in the back so you can place a candle inside it. There is no draft on the candle, so it will burn a long time. When you light it, it looks like magic."

Suddenly everyone is galvanized. We must have snow lanterns! Tasha tests the newly fallen snow. Perfect. We form an assembly line, making snowballs. Tasha constructs, passing on tricks of the trade as we give serious attention to our packing form. It is finished just as dusk falls. Someone fetches candles, and the lantern is illuminated. It does, indeed, look like magic, and as Tasha leans back from lighting the candle, a warm, otherworldly glow makes her seem enchanted and powerful. If there is a Queen of the Fairies, she is that queen. We applaud and she bows slightly, ill at ease with being the center of attention, but as aware of the magic as we are.

"I love snow. I love winter. It's such a nice, quiet time. There isn't the urgency of spring, summer, or fall to get the garden weeded or carrots put in the cellar. It's such a peaceful time. No wonder animals hibernate, because I think I slightly hibernate in winter. I get up much later in winter than I do the rest of the year."

Gingerbread Ornaments

Tasha's Christmas tree is justly famous for both its collection of family decorations and its handmade gingerbread ornaments. As with all aspects of Tasha's life, she manages to combine everyday activity with great artistry. Each gingerbread is truly an individual work of art. Unlike most of us, Tasha doesn't use cookie cutters to give shape to her ornaments. A lifetime of practicing her art has enabled Tasha to cut out her familiar animals freehand, sometimes barely looking at the dough. The shapes are linear and simple. The skill needed to turn them into creatures of fantasy is not.

Making the ornaments requires much rearranging of the kitchen and clearing of work areas. The dough has been made the evening before and chilled to make it sturdier as the shapes are cut.

Expectation abounds as the discussion turns to which animals to make. Tasha begins cutting out the form of a corgi, remembering previous ones. Her amazing eye and memory for detail enable her to recall if, twenty years earlier, one of the children or a friend made a particularly beautiful ornament.

Next she makes a duck, then a rabbit, followed in quick succession by another corgi, a sheep, a ram. The lines and the proportions are, naturally, accurate. A few go back into the bowl to be shaped again. One of the pleasures of making gingerbread ornaments is that you can recycle the dough until the results are satisfactory.

Tasha's corgyn, Rebecca and Owyn, settle blissfully by the wood stove. It is fiery hot, waiting to bake the ornaments to a honey golden brown. The dogs know the routine. This will be a nearly all-day affair. They bask in the warmth of the stove, ears cocking only when their names are mentioned.

Tasha's ornaments are quite well known. Museums have proudly exhibited them, and once, the White House called and persuaded her to make a special batch for Lyndon Johnson's Christmas tree.

The last bit of dough turned into art, Tasha begins baking the gingerbread. A delicious aroma fills the kitchen. The ornaments are not meant to be eaten — they have almost no taste. Even though we all know this, we enjoy the smell. Rebecca and Owyn take notice as well.

Once the cookies have baked and cooled, they are ready for decorating. A thick white frosting has been prepared while the ornaments were baking. Paper cornucopias are fashioned to hold the frosting.

Everyone takes a full cornucopia and begins. I immediately make a horse decidedly un-horse-like. Tasha is on her second figure, and the results are stunning. Soon we have frosting on the table and the floor, on clothing, and, to a greater or lesser degree, on the ornaments. Tasha, however, hasn't wasted a bit, and her gingerbread animals have become art. They are placed in the pantry to harden a bit more, poised for the moment when the tree is ready for them.

Afterward the gingerbreads were laid out on the long table, and Kitty made paper cornucopias to hold the white frosting so everyone had a chance to outline and decorate whatever he pleased. You had to be careful not to squeeze the cornucopia too hard, or else the frosting came out at the top. Of course it could be eaten, but it was more fun to make frosting feathers on ginger owls, or frosting scales on ginger fishes.

— *Becky's Christmas*

Tasha Tudor's
Christmas Tree Gingerbread

1 cup shortening	½ teaspoon ground ginger
1 cup light brown sugar	2¼ teaspoons salt
3 eggs, well beaten	1½ teaspoons baking soda
1½ cups molasses	1 teaspoon cinnamon
6 cups bread flour	

Cream the shortening and add the sugar, eggs, and molasses. Sift the remaining ingredients into the mixture. Chill, roll out, and cut into shapes for the tree. Bake on sheets at 350°F until dry but not crisp. Decorate with frosting (see below).

Frosting

1½ cups sugar	2 fresh egg whites
½ cup water	

Boil the sugar and water to spin a fine thread. Beat the egg whites in a separate bowl. When the syrup makes a fine thread, pour it over the egg whites and beat well. Make a paper cornucopia and force the frosting through onto the gingerbread.

The Animals' Christmas

All the creatures who live in and around Corgi Cottage add to its richness and energy, even though all is not completely harmonious most of the year. The chippehackies, Tasha's word for chipmunks, are the biggest bother to Tasha, often devouring her bulbs. Even they are forgiven at Christmas, however, and apples and birdseed are allocated for them, as well as for the wild birds who converge in great numbers and color upon Tasha's bird feeder.

As a special treat for the birds, Tasha mounts twin trees on either side of the backdoor entrance and decorates them with homemade doughnuts. The doughnuts must be hung quite high, as Rebecca and Owyn are as fond of them as the birds are.

Tasha's illustrations for *The Christmas Cat*, by her daughter, Efner Tudor Holmes, beautifully express her feelings about the comforts of home necessary for all living creatures and of the love and reverence Tasha feels that they are due. No Tudor Christmas would be complete without including them in the celebration.

With all the Christmas bustle in the winter kitchen, Minou, Tasha's famous one-eyed cat, finds a more peaceful spot on the bed in Tasha's loom room. The quilt, in appropriate Christmas colors, is one of Tasha's favorites.

All of Tasha's animals are important to her everyday life and serve as models for her art. Rebecca and Owyn, especially, are aware when they're being sketched or painted and have been known to hold a pose when requested.

At Christmas the animals are given special treats, special attention, and their own decorations. On Christmas Eve the hens and roosters might be given a special hot mash or fresh fruit. The goats will receive apples and the tenderest of hay, reserved only for treats. Owyn and Rebecca are given bones and home-made dog biscuits, and Puss receives catnip grown by Tasha. The wild birds who frequent Tasha's bird feeder are treated to a wide array of seeds, suet, and homemade balls of peanut butter, raisins, and chopped nuts. Doves, a universal symbol of peace that have fig-ured prominently in Tasha's Christmas cards, receive a special blend of their favorite feed, and the sparrows, finches, and other birds who live in Tasha's loom room are given seeds with flower blooms or a chicory salad, which they love. Hannah and Pegler, Tasha's African gray parrots, are treated to flowers from the greenhouse, fresh fruit, and seedcake.

One of Tasha's gentle jests is serving up Hannah on a platter just before the turkey appears. Guests are suit-ably startled, and Hannah rather enjoys the attention, not moving until she receives her signal from Tasha.

Charles Henry Cackleberry, one of Tasha's favorites, is always mindful of where he will appear to his best advantage.

Tasha's goats are important contributors to her larder. They are well cared for and enjoy a life unequaled by others of their species.

At Christmastime, the goat barn is decorated with greens and apples, which more often than not disappear quickly. Tasha's silver Nubians are more interested in food than in decoration. The holiday feeling of goodwill extends to all living things at Corgi Cottage and makes the Christmas celebration complete.

The Crèche

The crèche is one of the most important elements of a Tasha Tudor Christmas. It has evolved over half a century since Tasha first made her Madonna — a beautiful bisque doll with delicate features, dressed in simple clothes any young mother of modest means might wear. The infant Jesus is a small bisque baby doll Tasha had as a child. The rest of the crèche has become even more distinctly her own.

Tasha's approach to her family's crèche was symbolic, not representational of earlier, grander crèches reminiscent of Renaissance paintings of the Adoration. She wanted a simple manger scene her children could relate to and be a part of. The children contributed many of the animals as they grew up: a Steiff donkey, a rooster and hens, sheep, even a small rabbit. Tasha made a remarkable goat by first carving a wooden frame and then covering it with material from an old nightgown. At some point as the decades passed, a guardian elk joined worshippers, his origin lost in time. Even stranger, a small, unidentifiable creature appeared — somewhat otterlike — which no one can remember bringing to the crèche. The manger was fashioned from an old shingle.

Grannie had made the Madonna, also a long time ago. The figure was hard to set up just as Becky wanted her, but at last she bent lovingly over the small wooden manger and looked at the china baby. Becky made new halos for them of gold paper. There were a donkey, two black lambs and a white one, and a most adorable cock and hen. Becky especially loved them; it was like seeing old friends to have them come out of the Christmas box once more.
— Becky's Christmas

There was no requirement that things for Tasha's crèche be perfectly proportionate or that the animals be of a species which could actually have been present at the birth of Christ. It was only important that her family create, together, a representation of that special night long ago.

Tasha has set up two distinctly different crèches throughout the years, alternating between one and the other as circumstances dictate. She has used both scenes in her art, and both remain indelibly etched in the hearts of her fans.

The setting for the crèche most often used is a unique one. When her family was just beginning, they lived in a large farmhouse in New Hampshire. Tasha needed a place for the crèche where she could safely keep the children involved with it and still keep an eye on them. Since the large kitchen was the room most used, Tasha thought the Dutch oven the perfect choice. "It made a lovely stable, dark and mysterious, a sin-gle candle giving light to the manger scene." The children were enthralled, and a tradition that would be cherished in her work was born:

Becky was allowed to set up the crèche herself this year. The crèche was made in the brick oven beside the big old-fashioned fireplace where people used to cook when Becky's house was new, a long, long time ago, when America was new, too.

— *Becky's Christmas*

The other crèche site was much more dra-matic and more symbolic of the journey to find the Christ child. Perhaps a quarter of a mile from

Corgi Cottage, through winding woods, there juts out an outcropping of majestic stone with a great many nooks and crannies along its base. Tasha conceived the idea of placing the crèche in one of the small grottolike niches and then leading everyone on a candlelit quest through the woods in search of the birthplace of Jesus.

"When we moved to Vermont, we didn't have the Dutch oven built the first year, so I put the crèche out in the woods for that first Christmas. My granddaughter Laura was three, and it impressed her much more than the tree or anything else. All she wanted to talk about was 'the baby in the woods.' We liked it so much that we continued to have it there every year."

If the snows were unusually deep, the brick-lined bake oven to the left of the large fireplace in the winter kitchen at Corgi Cottage would be used. When a close family friend could

no longer make the journey through the woods, the indoor crèche was used for many years. It was there that one of Tasha's cats had her own religious experience. "I don't know if she was expecting a mouse to be in the straw or if she suddenly got religious, but the poor thing leaped right into it, badly singeing her whiskers in the process. Worse, when they grew out, they were crinkled, as if she had a permanent wave. She was mortified."

In recent years the crèche in the woods has been revived and is one of Tasha's most beloved traditions.

Preparations for the magical journey begin in the late afternoon of Christmas Eve. Once the crèche is in place, candles must be placed around  it and along the sides of the path, working backward from the crèche to the beginning of the woods. Usually Tasha and her son Tom perform this ritual, but one year the honor of helping fell to me. I moved slowly, partially because of a lack of experience and partially because I was savoring the experience. Tasha didn't seem to mind.

This year all is ready. The snows have been deep, and drifts make the going challenging. A few friends have been invited, and everyone has a candle to light the way. Tasha leads. We wend our way slowly through the deep forest. It is much darker now, and the tall trees block out the moonlight. Our candles light no farther than our next step, and the forest suddenly seems immense. We move slowly, staying close together, sharing the quest. We have become the shepherds, the wise men, on a symbolic journey in search of truth. The excitement is palpable.

We round a bend in the path and suddenly there is a distinct glow ahead of us. As we approach, the manger gradually comes into

focus, the center of a richly concentrated circle of light. Ageless and magical, the crèche at the base of the rocks seems to have been put there by other hands. Mounds of snow, intense darkness, towering trees, and huge slabs of rock firmly entrenched in the hillside form a mystical backdrop to the miracle we seek.

We form a semicircle. After a few audible gasps, there is silence. No one moves. We are transfixed. I pull my gaze away from the scene to look at Tasha. The spirit of a young girl radiates from her eyes. The woman who has given the world so much magic becomes ethereal in the glow from the small candles. I know at that moment what the true meaning of Christmas is. We all do. The "baby in the woods" has once again worked his miracle.

The trip back moves very quickly. The path has already been broken, and the search

has been successful. We are all elated. It really is Christmas!

Back at Corgi Cottage we gather in the winter kitchen, enjoying tea and cookies. We are reflective and grateful. We use this quiet time, full of small talk, to mask our growing anticipation of the coming day. The stockings are hung on the mantelpiece, the fire banked and covered, and we retire to our rooms, inviting visions of sugarplums to dance in our heads.

Stockings are hung at Corgi Cottage on Christmas Eve, in descending order of age. Their delights are the subject of much speculation and amuse both young and old throughout Christmas Day.

TASHA'S CHRISTMAS STOCKINGS

While the Tudor family gathers around the fireplace to open their Christmas stockings, beneath the floor-boards, a family of Tudor mice celebrate their Christmas by dancing around their own decorated tree ablaze with candlelight. Tasha's masterful blending of reality and magic — and they are actually one and the same at Corgi Cottage — makes this watercolor one of her best.

Christmas Dinner

Tasha is at her best when she's doing several projects at once. She has an uncanny ability to leave one task at the exact moment she is needed at another one. Watching her prepare Christmas dinner while decorating the tree and attending to other last-minute or just-thought-of surprises is astounding. One is immediately aware of an unusual quality Tasha gives to kitchen activities. She doesn't hurry. In fact, I don't believe I have ever seen her hurry. She has invented her own sense of time and, in so doing, is able to accomplish much more than most mortals. Not only does she not rush, she enjoys, relishes each moment of each task. "There! Isn't that fine!" she'll remark during some stage of food preparation that would be no more than another step to most people.

Tasha's Christmas dinner preparation is a joyful process, but it's also a lesson in history. Tasha's turkey is roasted — really roasted — in an antique tin kitchen that backs up to the fireplace and reflects its heat as the turkey is periodically hand turned on a long spit to guarantee that it's cooking evenly. Tin kitchens, also known as reflector ovens, are definitely from another century, and although one might see them occasionally in a museum, it's another thing entirely to watch one actually roast a turkey more expertly than any modern oven could ever achieve.

Grannie had stuffed the turkey the night before, and it was now brought from the cold front hall, where it had been placed for safekeeping, and put in the tin kitchen. Becky's family always cooked their turkey before the open fire in the tin kitchen instead of in an oven. It tasted wonderful. It was Becky's privilege to turn the spit every twenty minutes and to do the basting. George Pussy and the dogs took a great interest in the turkey-roasting and sat about the hearth in hopes of spilled drippings.

— Becky's Christmas

The process is slow, taking most of the day, and one that Tasha is particularly fond of. The tin kitchen itself was handed down in Tasha's family. "I rescued it! It still has its spits and ladle. I've never seen one with the ladle. It's a dandy!" The process is just the way Tasha prefers it, slow. The tin kitchen has a spout through which drippings are released, so an iron porriger must be watched carefully because Rebecca and Owyn are inordinately fond of the drippings, which Tasha uses to baste the turkey. The entire day becomes one of hope for the corgyn.

Tudor

THE TASHA TUDOR COOKBOOK

Tasha Tudor
THE TASHA TUDOR COOKBOOK
Recipes and Reminiscences from Corgi Cottage

Featuring More Than 80 of Tasha Tudor's
Favorite Family Recipes

Little,
Brown

While the turkey is roasting, everything else is prepared. Tradition and history continue as ironstone molds, yellow ware bowls, copper pans, and iron skillets all fulfill their intended purposes.

Tasha works on the side dishes. She fixes succotash, "We've always had it," mashed potatoes with cream cheese, and a cranberry mold that she is renowned for.

Mother had rolls rising in the woodbox because it was nice and warm there, and had just turned out a beautiful mold of cranberry sauce in the shape of an ear of corn. Turning out the mold was always a tense moment, and Mother gave a sigh of relief as it slid onto the blue Canton platter, perfect in every respect.
— Becky's Christmas

As she adds the fresh cranberries to the sauce, Tasha uses a test I haven't seen before. "I don't use a thermometer," she admits. "I test it by putting a silver spoon in. I stir it and hold up the spoon and when the drops stick together,

it has reached the jelly stage. I do all my jelly that way."

As I compliment her on the ironstone mold she is using, Tasha is reminded that she has a miniature version. It is doll-size. "We used to use this little corn mold for the dolls' Christmas dinner. For the turkey, we would have roast squab. It was quite something."

I profess astonishment that Tasha had been able to create such magical, meaningful Christmases for four children while, at the same time, re-creating the same celebration for the dolls. "We always cooked an entire dinner in miniature for the dolls' Christmas. When we had doll fairs, the children would raise miniature vegetables, tiny ears of corn, all sorts of things. We would try to pick them when they were as small as possible. That was fun!"

In the afternoon, the dolls put on their aprons and came to the kitchen to help with the party preparations. There were cookies to be cut with thimbles, small pies to be rolled, a pan of tiny biscuits and a small mold of jelly to be made. The dolls felt quite tired when everything was finally finished and put away. They went to bed in expectation of tomorrow.

— The Dolls' Christmas

As Tasha reminisces about preparing two Christmas dinners, she reminds me that because she has always painted from life, many of her hundreds of Christmas cards have been sketched while the activities they depict were actually taking place.

"When I was younger and had to work harder, I used to paint fifteen Christmas cards a year and then they'd choose twelve to print. I usually had a baby on my lap, which made it interesting. The babies are now all grown up, but in my sketchbooks and my mind's eye, they are forever young. I used to use my children and my neighbors' children as models for my Christmas cards. I could get the girls to pose from vanity, but I had to bribe the boys with chocolate."

Recipes that you've had before taste entirely different when Tasha prepares them. She uses only the best ingredients. For each dish there are fresh herbs, picked only minutes before they are used. Homemade butter and fresh goat's milk add a rich quality, as do her eggs, remarkable because of the care and feed she gives her fowl. Tasha's chickens have an enviable diet. Should a cake turn out not quite right, it goes to the hens, as does fruit, vegetables, and bread soaked in goat's milk.

Tasha has illustrated several cookbooks over the years, including *Betty Crocker's Kitchen Gardens* and the *New England Butt'ry Shelf Cookbook*. Her masterpiece, however, is *The Tasha Tudor Cookbook: Recipes and Reminiscences from Corgi Cottage*. Written and illustrated by Tasha, it is an indispensable resource for those who want to prepare food as it was meant to taste. Tasha shares her favorite recipes there and continues to pass on tips and observations to anyone interested.

The discussion of food preparation is an engrossing one for Tasha, as is solving related problems — hers or others'. I had never been able to make really good piecrusts, and I finally asked Tasha about it. I was sure I had followed her recipe to the letter. She made a sample crust as I watched, and then she had me make one. She agreed that I had followed all her directions. She thought for a moment and then touched my hand. "Here's your problem! Your hands are much too warm. Stick them in the freezer for a moment, then work as quickly as you can. Get a marble rolling pin and chill it also. You'll see a big difference." From that day on, I could, and do, boast about my piecrusts. Tasha was pleased she had supplied the solution to my problem.

The dinner preparation progresses nicely, interspersed with decorating the tree, and the time has been filled so agreeably that it's rather a surprise when everything is ready. Tasha has been basting the turkey for hours and professes satisfaction as the plump bird reaches perfection. "Simply unsurpassed!" she exclaims as she pulls out the skewers and removes the turkey from the tin kitchen. Owyn and Rebecca, thwarted throughout most of the day, see their chance at last and have a pre-Christmas dinner feast. Owyn is a master at removing any vestige of drippings from the tin kitchen. One Christmas when he was just a puppy, he managed to fit himself completely inside the tin kitchen, where he proceeded to leave not even a drop. Adulthood and many such feasts make that impossible now, but he still does a thorough job.

Tasha has little modesty about the bird. "It's truly roasted, you know. When you cook one in a regular oven, it's baked, not roasted. It doesn't taste the same. We had a summer party one year and someone wanted turkey. I realized I didn't know how to cook a turkey in an oven. I never had." She hands me a sample, and I instantly agree with her. Never had turkey tasted so succulent. I tell Tasha so, and she nods in agreement. "I've increased the sales for tin kitchens considerably. Once someone tastes my turkey, they begin looking for one."

The table has been laid according to custom and is reminiscent of many of Tasha's Christmas cards. A soft, turkey-red patterned tablecloth supplies the perfect backdrop to antique silver and blue and white Fitzhugh plates, used only for special celebrations. Green Bristol glass tumblers are brought out at the last minute, as are finger bowls. Making the finger bowls produce melodious sounds is a traditional part of a Tudor feast, and tonight will be no exception.

Tasha carves the turkey expertly, and plates are passed. Toasts are made, honoring the season and the company. In the green Bristol glasses, sparkling cider rivals the finest champagne.

The dinner is superb. Everything tastes better than it ever has before, everyone agrees. Even last Christmas at Corgi Cottage pales a bit compared with this. Second helpings pay homage to the feast and the cook.

Tasha begins the humming of the finger bowls. She sets off quite a concert as everyone joins in. The sound is pleasantly haunting. The meal is over, the past has been acknowledged and revered, and the present is satiated. It has truly been a meal to be remembered for years to come. The tree awaits.

These finger bowls were a part of every holiday. They were of thick green glass, and after dinner everyone wet the tips of his fingers and ran them round and round the edges of the bowls, making thereby wonderful singing vibrations without which Becky would have considered a Christmas or Thanksgiving dinner incomplete.

— *Becky's Christmas*

The Tree

Tasha insists on a fresh-cut Christmas tree from her very own woods. It must be freshly cut because it will be lit with real candles. From her own woods, because that is the time-honored, old-fashioned way. It also ensures that Tasha gets just the tree she wants: "I always pick it out so there will be no arguments."

In the afternoon Father hitched up Brown Dobbin to the sledge, and they all drove over to the Christmas Woods to get the tree. It was a beautifully bright afternoon; the shadows on the snow were as blue as the far hills, and the Christmas Woods looked like an enchanted forest with the snow-covered spruce trees shining in the sun. There were patterns in the snow where rabbits and birds had left their tracks. Becky noticed where a little mouse had run in and out, "looking for fir-cone seeds for his Christmas dinner," Kitty said.

It was always hard to decide which tree to take; one was too tall, another too slim, but Dan found a perfect one by the wall, and he and Father cut it down and put it on the sledge. The others brought along the leftover branches for decorations, and they returned to the house, Mother and Kitty on the Sledge, Becky astride Brown Dobbin, and Father and the boys walking alongside.

— *Becky's Christmas*

The Christmas tree was brought from the hemlock woods. Then one waited forever and forever while it was changed to a magic tree with shining balls and candles. — *Snow Before Christmas*

In past Christmases, when no single perfect tree could be found, two would be selected and, with a bit of trimming and fitting, skillfully entwined into one impressive tree. Tom Tudor is an expert at this, and I had marveled at his ingenuity the previous year. This year there would be a perfect one. It was cut at the last possible moment and, Tasha leading the way, proudly brought into Corgi Cottage late in the afternoon on Christmas Eve.

As always, the tree was put up in the center of the parlor. It was easy to find the place where it was to stand because, over the years, the usually too-tall trees have worn a small hole in the ceiling. The tree had to be securely anchored to the four corners of the room. The sturdiness of the tree is important because of the weight of some of Tasha's ornaments. A sheet was placed on the floor to catch dripping candle wax. Once basic preparations were complete, the parlor door was closed and it became forbidden territory.

The passage of time and the growing-up of children have altered some of the patterns of Tasha's Christmas schedule, but the traditions remain. No one is allowed to see the tree until early evening on Christmas Day. It must be twilight or darker for the candles to show the tree at its best. Christmases now are less pressured than in past years, when children, impatient for the magic, needed to be kept busy while Tasha decorated the tree.

One of the Tudor family's most unusual traditions, the dolls' Christmas, is recalled fondly by Tasha:

"When my children were small, I had to decorate the Christmas tree myself. I decided to have the dolls celebrate their own Christmas on Christmas Eve, complete with presents from them to the children. We even made a tiny tree for the dollhouse. While the children were helping the dolls celebrate, I decorated the tree. It kept the children busy and became a big event. Much anticipated. Their presents from the dolls along with their stockings, which they opened on Christmas morning, would keep them occupied most of Christmas Day. I could finish the tree and cook Christmas dinner."

As Tasha decorates the tree, I am impressed with the time and care given to the process. The sturdiness of the tree is once again checked. It is safe for Tasha's glass ornaments. Hers is surely one of the most impressive collections anywhere. It consists of large, hand-blown ornaments in the shapes of balls, acorns, pears, and clusters of grapes. These heavy balls are lined with brightly colored mercury and are weighty not only literally but with family history as well. Called kugels, they are the forerunners of modern Christmas balls. It is a genuine source of pride to Tasha that they have been handed down in her family intact since 1858. There are hundreds of them in dozens of shapes and sizes, all carefully used and cherished. They are impressive and scary at the same time. Irreplaceable, they must be handled with the utmost care. Tasha knows them all by heart and places them carefully, some "where they've always been."

Next the gingerbread ornaments that proclaim the tree to be Tasha Tudor's are hung. The tree is somewhat full already, but there is much more to add: Danish woven hearts and straw decorations in a variety of shapes, birds, strings of glass beads, traditional clear toys, and many one-of-a-kind decorations collected over the years. When they were young, all of Tasha's children looked forward to the arrival of the clear toys, a gift each year from friends in Pennsylvania.

In the package were the Clear Toys, little figures made of barley sugar. They came in red, green, and pale yellow; this last color Becky liked best.

Mother put the box on the table. Kitty brought the large silver tray; then she and Dan and Ned and Becky unpacked them. It was fun to see what you unwrapped. There were several kinds of birds; there were trumpets, boats, pitchers, reindeer, and goats and monkeys and funny men. There were elephants too, and ponies with flowing manes of barley sugar, and cannon and a pipe for Father and Dan. Ribbons had to be tied to all of them so they could be hung on the tree. This job took all evening, but it was fun, and any broken toys could be eaten on the spot.

— *Becky's Christmas*

The tree is finished, but there is no haste. The candles are in place, but not lit. Not yet. Presents from Tasha are placed under the tree, awaiting the formal revealing of the tree. No one will be allowed in the parlor until dinner is finished. Only then can the rich spectacle of the tree be enjoyed. The tree waits; everyone anticipates.

With dinner finished, the conversation turns immediately to the tree. Past trees are remembered, as are gifts. Everyone has a favorite

memory to share. Mine is an enormous Steiff teddy bear given me by Tasha the previous year. It reminds me of one in a photograph of Tasha at her third birthday party, surrounded by dolls, bears, and other stuffed animals. While paying attention to the conversation, everyone clearly is listening for the music announcing that it is time for Tasha to present the tree.

The parlor door traditionally opens to the rich notes of "Hark! the Herald Angels Sing" played by an antique music box handed down in Tasha's family. It is rarely heard otherwise, so the music, sounding strangely formal, ceremonial, is a delight.

The first notes are struck, and Tasha proudly opens the parlor door and beckons everyone in. The candlelight is soft and brilliant at the same time and envelopes the room. Before I give myself over completely to the pleasures of the tree, dozens of watercolors run through my mind, depicting this exact scene. Life and art become one. A strange and dreamy state permeates the room. We are all inside one of Tasha's paintings, yet living the experience at the same time. Everything seems to be in slow motion for just a second, then joy mounts to a point where it can't be contained further and the room erupts in gasps of delight. Fantasy is made real. Everyone talks at the same time, moving around the massive tree. It cannot be taken in all at once. The decorations have great depth — layer upon layer of beautiful, treasured objects. Tasha touches ever so slightly one of her favorite ornaments, a tiny golden acorn. The touch is almost a caress. She smiles and gently taps a small silver bell nearby. "The sound of that bell forever makes me think of Christmas. Even in midsummer, I immediately see the Christmas tree."

Everyone explores the tree, anxious not to miss a single piece of the complex whole. The candles suffuse everything and everyone in a most flattering light. Kept upright by a weighted ball at the bottom of the holders, they give the tree a beauty no electric lights ever could.

Tasha's gingerbread animals take on a life of their own once they've been hung. The tree seems to be theirs, everything else is there only to properly accentuate them. Their proportion to the massive tree is perfect.

The kugels are breathtaking. They reflect the candlelight, themselves, and all of us. They appear to be tiny worlds, too deep to peer into beyond the surface. Although they have graced Tudor trees for 140 years, it would be difficult to imagine that they have ever looked better than tonight.

The wealth of ornamentation seems endless: papier-mâché fruit, blown-glass icicles, tiny birds, cornucopias filled with candy and tiny surprises, and quaint little gold-wire curlicues.

Tasha compares the tree favorably with its predecessors and recalls her first memory of a

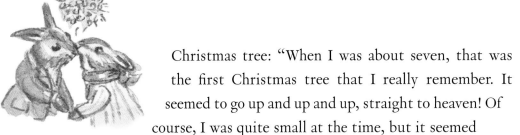

Christmas tree: "When I was about seven, that was the first Christmas tree that I really remember. It seemed to go up and up and up, straight to heaven! Of course, I was quite small at the time, but it seemed immense, tremendously tall, like a skyscraper."

So does this one to me. As I finally look up at the top, I see another uniquely Tasha Tudor touch. Crowning the tree is a large, black velvet raven, made by Tasha many years ago, in homage to the legend that the raven was the herald of Christ's birth. According to the story, a raven was flying over Bethlehem when he encountered a sky filled with angels. He was given the honor of announcing the birth of Christ to all the other birds. Inspired by the legend, Tasha made her raven, and he has been the finishing touch to her tree for decades.

Everyone enjoys the tree enthusiastically. It seems as if we are all in never-never land. We are children again, or at least completely comfortable with our childlikeness. I realize that this is exactly what many trees might have looked like a century or more ago — not just hung with the old ornaments, but imbued with a spirit of a far different time.

Gifts are exchanged and admired. Tasha reads "The Night Before Christmas" to us from one of her own versions. It is tremendously comforting to sit around Tasha's tree and have her read this Christmas classic to us, as she did years ago to her children, as her father did even more years ago to her. The past and the present seem to merge, as they often do at Corgi Cottage. All the Christmases past become a seamless part of this Christmas.

Soon after, Tasha gives notice that the candles have burned long enough. We sigh contentedly, try to take it all in one more time, then watch as Tasha extinguishes them one by one. We follow each candle's smoke as it streams upward. The room is getting darker and darker. We continue to stare, even after their glow has faded, as one would at the exact spot where one had seen fairies or Santa Claus. Magic must be honored.

Becky could hardly bear to leave when it was bedtime, but bedtime comes even on such wonderful days as Christmas.

Good nights and many thanks and hugs were exchanged all round, and soon the entire family had gone to bed.

Becky lay and listened to the stillness and watched the moonlight shining through the frosty window panes.

It's shining in on my dolls' house too, she thought, and on the Christmas tree. Then in her mind she saw the doll father and mother taking the doll children to see the big tree; how tremendous it would look in dolls' eyes. Then they would go to see the calendars, and last of all they would climb up over the small settle, probably by way of the stack of firewood behind it, and they would see the crèche, and the doll mother would be telling the doll children that Christmas first started when a real little baby boy was put in a manger in a place far, far away, called Bethlehem. . . and with this Becky fell asleep. — *Becky's Christmas*

Santa Claus

"My concept of Santa Claus came mostly from 'The Night Before Christmas.' We always read it out loud."

For many people, Santa Claus and his yearly visit to a particular household are an essential part of Christmas. To a large extent, our collective concept of Santa has the same origin as Tasha's, the classic poem "The Night Before Christmas."

Originally composed for his own children's entertainment by Clement Clarke Moore in 1822, the poem did not appear in book form until 1848. This account of a magical visit from Saint Nicholas transformed him from a religious figure to the secular Santa Claus we know today and made him a more universal, accessible character. He now represented the spirit of giving at Christmas, and every household was included.

Over the next century, hundreds of artists illustrated Moore's poem, each interpreting Santa more in the fashion of their time than in the spirit of its creator.

Tasha followed this same path, but having illustrated this Christmas classic three times, her depiction of Santa Claus has evolved with each new edition. The first, done more than thirty years ago, is a small, leatherbound volume that has gone on to become quite a collector's item. Though Santa is still presented relatively close to the usual concept, in this first depiction, Tasha begins to make Santa her own creation.

More than a decade later, Tasha once again illustrated Clement Clarke Moore's beloved poem, and the result is quite different. This Santa is decidedly more elfin and arrives with more than just enough magic to come down the chimney. Mice holding matches aloft like torches guide him to the rooftop. An owl serves as navigator. Amid a profusion of toys brought to life, Santa dances with one of Tasha's corgyn while Puss plays the fiddle. The corgi tries Santa's pipe, and a doll and jester dance, as does a catnip mouse.

Tasha had now clearly homed in on magic as the key element necessary to believe in Santa Claus. She depicted it beautifully, in an innovative, lively manner. Evaluating the work years later, Tasha reflects: "I was a lot younger then, and while different, it was probably more what people expected. A fat Santa Claus with a red suit."

Several decades later Tasha has once again illustrated the classic, this time producing a definitive version. It is painterly and truly magical. Santa is presented almost as a spirit, with slightly less than concrete form. He appears almost as light itself. He is a Santa one could believe in as a child and continue believing in into adulthood. He is, quite literally, the spirit of Christmas.

All of the other attendant Tasha Tudor magic is present, beautifully executed by a painter at the peak of her talent, incredibly in control of the paper, the paint, the inspiration. This new version contains some of the most richly detailed illustrations of her career.

Visions of sugarplums are mouthwatering, a corgi with a trumpet heralds Santa's arrival, and a cat and an owl help Santa fill the stockings. Each page is filled with classic Tasha Tudor inspiration and whimsy at its best.

Throughout, rich, vibrant color radiates from every page, while light is depicted in a softly realistic manner. Tasha considers it her best work.

"This one is more mysterious, and made all at night, which is the way Clement Clarke Moore thought of it. This is the best one I've done. Moore describes Santa as an elfin creature dressed in fur from his head to his foot, covered with ashes and soot. I've remained true to that."

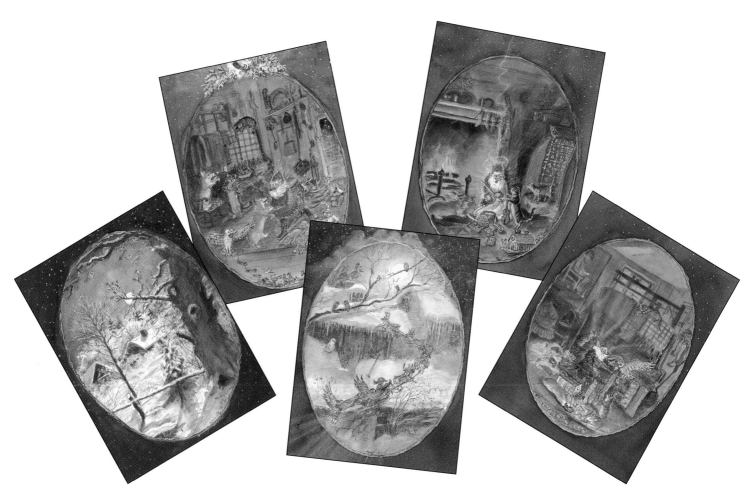

"THE NIGHT BEFORE CHRISTMAS"

This image shows a young mother wearing Tasha's own homespun apron and knitted shawl reading from one of Tasha's versions of "The Night Before Christmas" to a rapt audience. Tasha's legendary borders are well represented here by a delightful array of toys, gifts, and holiday treats.

Sleigh Ride

The tree is gone, the decorations carefully packed away in the attic. Leftovers have been turned into casseroles and soups, and newly received gifts are beginning to feel comfortable, part of the normal daily order. Christmas is technically over, at least by the calendar, but this is Corgi Cottage. The spirit of Christmas still lingers. In past years, when the children were small, an elaborate party would be held on the day after Christmas for the children's friends as a finale to the dolls' Christmas. It was enormously popular, and guests looked forward to it all year.

The tree would be lit one last time, and the dolls' Christmas decorations and gifts would be on display. A literary contest was part of the festivities, and each child brought an entry to the party. The judges weren't aware of the identity of the authors, so the judging was quite fair. The prize would be a coveted book with fine illustrations, often by Edmund Dulac, whom Tasha greatly admires.

After refreshments came Tasha's favorite part of the evening, a performance the Tudor family would have worked on since June, one of their marvelous marionette shows. "The marionette shows were originally conceived as entertainment for the dolls. We thought theater was what they needed."

The entire family participated in the shows. As many as forty different marionettes might be used in a single performance. *Little Red Riding Hood*, *Jack and the Beanstalk*, *The Bremen Town Musicians*, and *The Rose and the Ring* were among the lavish productions.

One of Tasha's favorites was *Sir Lancelot and the Dragon of Corbin* from *Le Morte d'Arthur*. "Seth made a wonderful silver dragon out of aluminum

foil. It was very pliant and connected. It had a pouch in its mouth that we filled with charcoal dust and a red silk tongue. Tom would lie under the stage and blow through an attached straw, and the dragon would blow these clouds of smoke, and its red tongue would come out. It was very fine. We even had a tournament be-tween Lancelot and another knight. The children loved it!"

Tasha's face becomes animated as she describes the performance, and she smiles at the end, happy in the memory. The past has been honored; today must now be lived. Tasha decides that the final touch, the send-off of this

Christmas into the New Year, should be a sleigh ride. It is the perfect idea.

Tasha's wide circle of friends includes experts on every conceivable subject, and sleigh rides are no exception. Two of her friends, Jill and Carl Mancivalano, own the Adams Farm, a working family farm passed down through six generations in Jill's family. They are devoted to sharing farm life with people who are attracted to a simpler pace but know little of the details. A variety of activities are presented throughout the year, including feeding and interacting with friendly farm animals, experiencing hands-on farm activities, milking goats, watching maple syrup being made, and taking hay rides in the fall and sleigh rides in the winter. With so many shared interests, Tasha looks forward to seeing them, and we know the conversation will be lively.

A phone call is made, and we are on our way. Their farm isn't far, but going there seems quite an adventure because we haven't left Corgi Cottage for some time. Jill and Carl are waiting for us, and an immense Belgian draft horse is already hitched to a sleek cabriolet sleigh from the 1880s. Carl dons his trademark coachman's attire, and we fill the sleigh and are off. Jill will join us midway at the lodge.

The air is brisk and clear, and we are all in high spirits. Forget the four-wheel-drive vehicle that enables us to navigate Tasha's difficult drive — this is the way to travel! We glide over the snow as if in another time, the sleigh bells resounding with music as pure as the bright, cold snowscape. We pass woods where maple sugar will soon be tapped. Higher up the trail, the forest is breathtaking, untouched except for the variety of animal tracks Carl points out. He is an excellent guide. His stories are charming, and each local landmark is described with appropriate detail and embellished, perhaps, a bit. No matter. Actually, it's exactly what we want. Not facts, but swift and entertaining passage toward the New Year.

Tasha is enchanted. This ride, this day, this Christmas, are all to her liking. She radiates satisfaction.

By the time we reach the lodge, we are reveling in the experience. Jill has prepared tea and gingerbread with lemon sauce. Both are delicious, and we savor them and the moment. Jill and Carl's daughter, Olivia, naps nearby. The horse waits patiently in front of a blind so he won't be distracted. Everyone is content. Tasha gives the ultimate compliment to the ride: "It makes one purr with pleasure."

Back in the sleigh, we begin the descent. It has been a perfect day, a perfect farewell to a perfect Christmas. The ride ends, but the memory and the contentment linger as we return to Corgi Cottage.

*T*asha has a final gift for us. We have tea in front of a roaring fire in the winter kitchen. As we drink from her trademark blue and white soft-paste teacups and finish the last of her mincemeat cookies, she shares with us one of her favorite quotations. It contains a philosophy that has guided her life. It is as familiar to us as it is to her, yet we never tire of it. Hearing her read the words we know to be true, they seem truer than ever:

> *I salute you! There is nothing I can give you which you have not; but there is much that, while I cannot give, you can take.*
>
> *No heaven can come to us unless our hearts find rest in it today. Take Heaven.*
>
> *No peace lies in the future which is not hidden in this present instant. Take peace.*
>
> *The Gloom of the world is but a shadow; behind it, yet within our reach is joy. Take Joy!*
>
> *And so, at this Christmas time, I greet you, with the prayer that for you, now and forever, the day breaks and the shadows flee away.*
>
> FRA GIOVANNI
> A.D. 1513